Contents

In My Room 1
Memory in a Dream 2
The Edge 3
Tempo 4
Traversing the Peninsula 5
On the Other Side 6
Freedom Tastes Like Saltwater 7
Amethyst in the Morning 8
On My Farm 10
Drops of Red 11
When the Sun Cools Down 12
Honey Bees 13
Numbers 14
Jardin de Suenos 15
Bootjack 16
Sounds on the River 17
Glassine Fragments 18
Windswept 19
On a Wire 20
A Warm Day in Winter 21
A Walk at Sunrise 22
Traffic Dancing 23
Dripping Time 24
Letters in a Word 25
Meditation 26

Letters That Aren't Sent 27
A Whirl 28
Moving Water 29
What Is Red? 30
Forgotten Moon 31
Growing Older 32
In Our Own Way 33
Journey 34
Waiting for Thunder 35
December 36
Acknowledgements 37

*To Barbara
a fellow poet & new
friend...*

On a Wire

by *Joy!*

Dianne Elizabeth Butler

Dianne Butler

DORRANCE PUBLISHING CO., INC.
PITTSBURGH, PENNSYLVANIA 15222

The contents of this work including, but not limited to, the accuracy of events, people, and places depicted; opinions expressed; permission to use previously published materials included; and any advice given or actions advocated are solely the responsibility of the author, who assumes all liability for said work and indemnifies the publisher against any claims stemming from publication of the work.

Portrait picture of Dianne by Megan Eden. Cover photo and art by Dianne Butler.

All Rights Reserved
Copyright © 2012 by Dianne Elizabeth Butler

No part of this book may be reproduced or transmitted, downloaded, distributed, reverse engineered, or stored in or introduced into any information storage and retrieval system, in any form or by any means, including photocopying and recording, whether electronic or mechanical, now known or hereinafter invented without permission in writing from the publisher.

Dorrance Publishing Co., Inc.
701 Smithfield Street
Pittsburgh, PA 15222
Visit our website at *www.dorrancebookstore.com*

ISBN: 978-1-4349-1448-4
eISBN: 978-1-4349-1363-0

Dedication

This book is dedicated to my mother Minnie F. Butler who brought to me the passion for reading.

In My Room

Lines weave, reflecting in mirrored glass shapes
of faces, orbs, square jars and vases,
sculptures transparent as the arched window
that lets in the dawning light.
Spirits of icons guard the walls,
a Buddha, a bell, a picture from the past
in black and gray.

Incense of cinnamon and sandalwood,
mourning light where the full moon rises
to the sound of a crying wind on the river.
A storm chases low clouds
across the fresh soil,
green of spring sprouting
surprises the tearing sky.

Memory in a Dream

I dream of a big wooden house,
falling apart, boards unpainted,
lichen covering the walls gray-green.
I enter slowly, careful to find
the planks that won't cave in.
The sea laps at the foundation,
froth and foam lick the splintered walls.
I whisper through my fear, an oral disclosure
to spirits I sense around me.
I hear the voices of the sea
slapping the structure of fear,
the source like a river, washes memory away.
I feel the spirit, it is benevolent,
the inflorescence of flowers
in the density of my life
is awakened in that house,
becoming new,
smelling of sandalwood that burns at sunrise.

The Edge

At the edge of the storm flies the albatross,
searching the sky for the slipstream
that will carry it home.

At the edge of the maelstrom the flotsam
is caught in an eddy, circling, circling.

At the edge of the hurricane cumulous clouds
climb carrying lightning and thunder, hail and winds
that scale back the tides.

At the edge of the grassfire the antelope run
with the rabbits leaping away to distant hills.

At the edge of the controversy
the earth is consumed
by the industrial age chewing at its core
like the hungry animal it is.

Tempo

Peacocks yawp across the river,
cottonwoods and gnarled oaks echo whispers.
The north wind blows the chimes on the porch
raising clacks and taps, dancing
through fingers of air juggling the weight of them.
Ions circle up and down in jubilation outside
the tall windows of an old house
open in the night to hear silent waves
slide beneath the sound of darkness;
insects playing cellos and violins,
an orchestra in the lush grass lifting
spring away from winter.
I keep the tempo
as time drifts coldly past.

Traversing the Peninsula

I touched the sea and it touched me.
The Sunrise Motel in the morning,
the Sunset Motel at night,
and in between I walked with the wind,
sand blowing patterns in
white and grey and brown.
The cold wrapped my ankles,
the numb running up my thighs,
anchoring me there
in the low tide of winter.

On the Other Side

Around her neck a white scarf flutters
like a dove struggling for freedom
as she drives the tiny slate blue car
as fast as the curving mountain roads
will allow. The air is chill, winter nearing
spring. There are lime green buds on the trees,
the angry wind rushes across her ears.
She's heading to the rustic cabin,
running away from family and feuds.
Why does it always seem the red clay road
out is longer than the same road in?

On the other side is the Pacific Ocean.
The eagle sails on the cloud,
slips through and disappears, diving
headlong to the roiling sea, breaking hard,
spreading the broad span of its wings,
snatching the silent shivering moon.

Freedom Tastes Like Saltwater

A hat on the bed making claim
to my life. His hat, a baseball cap
with a logo of his business bright
over the bill. "Andy's Landscaping,"
it read. I'd hired him one day—
the first in the yellow pages.

After the divorce I felt free and light.
He didn't want to leave,
the yard was perfect,
his garden full of fruit,
but I'd tasted the sea,
and it offered freedom.

Amethyst in the Morning

The wedding of Topaz and Matthew was in Baltimore, Elayne mentioned in her journal about the ginger colored dresses of the bridesmaids, a streamlined design done in good taste. It had been a wonderful occasion.

After that wedding, she'd gone to Europe and ridden the Orient Express. Its flimflam sound of the wheels destroyed her concentration. Her mind went back to the days in Canada with her young husband; the ocean scene with the tusk of the walrus on shore gleaming as it chewed on the endive-like seaweed.

When she arrived in Paris, it was February and the weather was like spring. She wanted to take a hot-air balloon ride over the Eiffel Tower, just as she'd done back in 1966 before she was married. The aerosol sound of the balloon being filled had made her tingle with excitement. But that was the end of a beginning.

The year she left her husband of twenty years, she flew to Budapest, participated in a commune, and formed a frame she could live by at any moment. The longer she was there, the more she knew what the real trash in her life was.

She had made good friends with two other women. They became like three on a match, burned bridges behind them as they traveled and went back to the states, settling in Missouri, "the show me state." They found it to be the root of evil, separating them with a shiver. A shamble of arguments extended until they began wearing earplugs. The only good thing about Missouri is the rhubarb, but even then, the leaves are poisonous.

She left the other women and floated above the highways into Brazil. The tranquil, somber heat of the tropics was elementary to her. There was not a rude person around and she felt at once that she began to really find herself. She thought, *The only thing I need is a watercolor world that changes on its own, bringing me the surprise of chrysanthemum days. I can live on mutton and bark if I have that.*

In that ancient home in Brazil, the flight of swifts from a chimney caught her eye, made her think of Fresno, and the day she was married. She still believed in Jesus back then, saw the miracle of him in the ice cream melting down her arm.

She stood at a south-facing window, a shot glass full of absinthe in her hand. She'd just gotten a letter from her ex and was wondering how he found her. It is an unequivocal mystery, a sequel to the way he seemed to find her anywhere.

There were seven horses beside the fence, cork trees atop the mountains in the distance, and amethyst in the morning light. The telephone rang and the voice of her aunt in Kansas surprised her. She remembered the triangles and squares of the fences around her aunt's place, the oleander that poisoned a dog which slept under it too often, and the swan that chased her across the dirt yard.

Her aunt, who didn't believe in divorce, whispered, "Your mother passed on yesterday. I called your husband."

It was the first death so close to home, a season to endure in the still air. After hanging up, she reached into her rusty file cabinet to find her passport. It was time to head north.

What she found in Kansas was like a blast zone, twenty-five cars sat around the juniper trees when she arrived. She had to sip from her tiny bottle of absinthe daily just to get by. Her reward was also her punishment. Blossoming into a rage, she zoomed through the rituals, saying her good-byes on that grassy knoll, then finding herself standing in front of the open refrigerator, staring at all those casseroles.

She gazed out the window, her view clouded with tears. The birds of North America flitted through the oleander, and landed in the juniper. Her face was florid, a belated sign of loss and remembrance. There was a sympathy card from her husband. She thought as she took another sip from the flask, *Yes, I guess absinthe does seem to make the heart grow fonder.* And she began laughing uncontrollably until she began to sob.

End

On My Farm

I look out my window, watching
the green John Deere tractor
glide up and down,
through the rows of sprouting lettuce.
Rough clods of rich dark soil,
the earth incumbent with nutrient
wafts lightly into my room;
mushroom, worms, silt
from years gone past—
flooding rivers until the levees,
canals and ditches reclaim the land.
I'm learning what it takes to build a dream.

Drops of Red
(For my father, Leslie)

Running through a field of ochre wheat,
I see Daddy driving the dusty green combine.
My hair is burned blonde by the hot summer sun.
He reaches down with grain dusted arms,
lifts me up to the massive machine,
lets me ride in the metal bin behind him.
Wheat fills around my skinny brown legs.
The dust smells of toasted flour, new
as the day, young as the child I am.
Daddy tries to dump the harvest,
when he discovers I'm trapped;
a billion fingers of grain grasping my body,
claiming me for their own.
He tugs in desperation, every farm accident
rolling like a horror film through his mind.
He has to flip the auger switch a touch, a tap…
to drop a half bushel before I twist
into the sharpened screw.
He yanks me once more and I'm tugged free
but for my red shoes tumbled
like the chaff pulled along the blade,
the harvester rumbles, grinding,
dropping, one-two, red spots onto the hill of gold.
Daddy retrieves the solemn evidence,
examines the scarred soles.
He walks toward me, sloughing
through the stubble, whispering, muttering.
His hands are rough, his touch tender
as he rubs each of my dirty feet
before slipping on those shoes
and tying the laces tightly.

When the Sun Cools Down

White cranes roost in the cottonwoods.
Their flight at twilight is graceful;
long flowing feathers glide
as the wings slowly push the air
and they soar, turn, reaching
for the branches rustling in the breeze.
It's a nervous time, an awkward grace
as the limber branches dip and sway
with the weight of the large white birds.
They struggle each evening for a toehold,
sometimes missing altogether, and again
the wings spread wide to keep from falling
to the flowing green water of the Sacramento.
They've been fishing all day, stalking crayfish
on dirt banks, canals, and irrigation ditches,
and like the farmers who work in the fields,
it's been a long dry day and it's time to roost
when the sun cools down to twilight.

Honey Bees

Where the best red clover grows
unattended across the mountain meadows,
blossoms turn the hillsides
into a blush of burgundy.
Honey, that golden molasses,
oozing from the hives,
the hum like ohms of a Dalai Lama.
The bees grow insistent
protecting their queen,
they sing to her
a tupelo honey song.

Numbers

5
Five gray doves sit on the wire
coo-cooing their mewing sound,
a pleasant comma in the sentence of living.

16
Sixteen white egrets
nest in the swaying cottonwoods
across the meandering river.

25
Twenty-five paper wasps drink muddy water
from the dog's plastic bowl
filled by a drip—dripping faucet.

50
Fifty gophers burrow around me,
mounds of fresh dark soil
hills the lawn and bark strewn mulch.

64
Sixty-four years doesn't stop me
from shoveling dirt, soil to grow
food that feeds the neighborhood.

Jardin de Suenos

The pump is pushing water to the plum orchard,
interrupting the quiet as the southern breeze
accompanies a birdsong chorus.
I helped stretch the garden fence between
the redwood posts today, and
wrote *Jardin de Suenos* on the archway of the gate:
spaghetti squash, watermelon, cantaloupe, turnip,
carrots, cucumbers, tomatoes, yellow and green squash,
orange and yellow marigolds, and sunflowers;
everything young, yet growing,
filling in the scars of planting.
The irrigation pump roars, surrounding the croaks
of a thousand frogs mating in the moonlight.
Hot of day, cool of night, dust floats as motes
of sun and starlight.
It sets on my tabletops and floor.

Bootjack
(For Judy Fitzpatrick)

My favorite riding boots
are well worn,
stepped in horse manure
too many times
while saddling a spooky cayuse.
After a hard day's ride
those boots are like
a second skin
protecting tender toes.

Those boots fit so well
I have to use the antique bootjack
I keep under my bed
just to prove there's something
else besides those boots
keeping me upright.

Sounds on the River

No human sounds come from the river, only
the rustling ribbon of leaves on the other side.
But then a whoop-whooping takes over,
a red Sikorsky helicopter, a tether hanging down
like a dragonfly with a broken tail.
I watch as it splashes something into the river
while rising sharply and banking away.
I sniff the air, wondering if they've dropped
a lethal spray to kill bugs or fungus
or whatever enemy some bureaucrat might imagine.
There is no odor.
The stuttering thump of the giant grows,
and dips to the water, so low I can only see
circling blades above the golden grass
that covers the levee.
I now see the tether is a hose
as they siphon, then dump, practicing
for the next wildfire they will squelch.

Glassine Fragments

California summer burns into fall,
days cooling, winds whipping
willow limbs to the ground.
The light hits the levees,
sprouting green after the first
heavy rainstorm.
The new lawn glows florescent
as glassine fragments glisten
and mushrooms explode white in mounds.
Wood smoke slips into the air,
sneaking into my open door in the night.
The roof drips with morning dew
as the fog fades; the day turning
slowly pink to mauve.
as I toss the covers from my bed,
and rise once more,
a day to toil out of doors,
pretending that summer
has only just begun.

Windswept

The autumn moon
drops stars onto the fields,
fresh earth churned warm
under twilight air
cooling the dew,
grown fresh after
a windswept storm.
Spectral light slides sideways,
in a misshapen fall to winter way.
I turn my wicker chair east as
the full ripe orange rises
above the horizon
of indigo ridged Sierras.

On a Wire

The red tailed hawk sits on a wire
staring down at the ground.
There's a rodent or, perhaps, a snake
among the rustling, quaking grasses.

They wait, still, and they wait,
hoping the other will move first.
The hawk dives from the sky,
talons extended,
a skittering is made through the wet weeds.

The mandarin moon sinks,
sliding over the horizon;
oozing the fall equinox,
through the tender snoring night.

On a wire I wait,
skitter through the days
of the autumn vanilla moon
as it melts into its icy winter way.

A Warm Day in Winter

The moon sits like a teacup
catching feathered snow,
reflecting light ocher clouds,
all grounded in air.
I taste the lemon tang of spring
on that January day,
particles melt on my tongue
catching the false warmth.
The sun touches a breeze, rippling
waves, lifting the fine hair
on my freckled arms,
my bare toes are cold as crystal ice cubes.
Winter, a surprise when the snow
doesn't fly from the sky
and sun kisses your cheeks rose.

A Walk at Sunrise

In the forest of my dreams
cedar kisses the damp air,
oxalis grows like castles on the moss-laden
limbs of the white barked alder.
Slow footsteps crackle the sound
through leaves, so wet they stick
to my bare feet.

The fog is thinning
and the sun makes an attempt
to spread the clouds wide.
The mist enwraps me in its gauzy curtain
and my hair hangs white in wispy tendrils
as I bend to smell the wild bleeding hearts
that tickle my nose,
but the color gives me no sweet aroma
as they stand sentry among the lichen covered stones.

Traffic Dancing

I hear the music of traffic dancing past
in tango rhythms, concert of tones
in timpani, horn, reeds,
and electronic song.
There's charcoal colored pavement
slashing the green page of the valley floor,
half notes in yellow and white divide.
Drivers turn and weave in cars,
and trucks, and motorcycles,
a cotillion reel at an intersection.
I wonder where they will all go
when the last dance is done?

Dripping Time

I feel so unattached here
across the nation, away
from family and home.
under the dark rain
dripping time away,
I miss them.
I wonder why my psyche
struggles with freedom.
The change is work, a labor for myself
It is a selfish chore.
I paint pictures, write, explore
the Atlantic beach finding
only eastern sand and sea
spreading out before me.

Letters in a Word

In the quarter light of my cell I write about it all.
Sensing the words, I see the pictures
in my head as I caress the keys.

It is like a new love, this laptop.
I work with letters, learning through touch
spent in the quiet dark of late night.

It is like those first times with you, my new love.
We learn the letters of each other,
write passionate words and stories with no plot.

The moon is on the wax, glimmering off the Sound
and there you are again,
as the keys lie quiet with the page.

Meditation

Sound echoes in a vast hollowness
of the rooms where I meditate
on memories that once were ours.
French doors radiate broken cloud light.
There is an empty place on a sunbathed
balcony that holds your shape.
On occasion I touch you and
it is like an echo coming home.
I feel you there near the fireplace,
the light licking your skin.
It never mattered how many rooms
our houses might hold
only that we are in them together.

Letters That Aren't Sent

Truths in life are a smoky cloud
that disappears in the slightest breeze.
I want to write that book with you,
combine people left at home with those
that had to go, explore connections
and the separate side of what life is like.
There are possibilities molded in your form,
roses delivered, but not taken.
I planted a flower seed that didn't grow
on the edge of change and watched from a distance
in the tightest of fringes, gave audience to an idea
and worked outward, trying to understand.
I remember striding side by side with you,
hips touching, steps the same.
We are no different now,
just letters that are no longer sent.

A Whirl

Sleeping under a whirling fan
it click-clicks the breeze,
stirring air to cool bare shoulders
in the warm sullen air of the honey
summer night that's come to the northwest,
full of sunflower and lavender days.
The changing tides with the moon's butter light
upon the gleaming sea has a salty scent
that tickles with the tang of it.
In August aril dreams, the wind licking
my sunburned neck is like you
whispering my name.

Moving Water

In your far land, with your singular ocean,
a full moon rises over ships afloat
on the moving water that holds you solely.
I am here alone singing songs by firelight,
strumming a tune on my scarred guitar.
I find agates flaming when the sun
catches their clear curved edges.
The dark lines run deep and I wonder
how you are, who you are, on that distant sea,
that ocean that can never really be yours
because its icy depths belong to no one.

What Is Red?

Is it the pink in the sunset on a cloudy
twilight evening, sanguine, a sober moment?
Or, perhaps, the rendezvous with a secret lover,
a tryst from midnight to dawn?
The reds in life may be the high
or the low, raised by passion
or pushed under like the tides
drowning those who come too close.

Red zooms me to heights
of gaiety when I put the top down
of the convertible and burn
my face in the summer sun
and winter wind;
freedom brushing across
my frozen ears
as a smile
bends my red lips.

Forgotten Moon

A forgotten moon nests in a chimney
near the red glass sea
shedding its yellow silken jacket.
The yellow-red scents the panes
of the ramshackle house
where the glimmering smoke rises
like a wavering white stick.
The mountain rocks the nesting swallows
locked in the flowering silent thorns.
A wind wafts the scent of smoke
back down the chimney
while an old couple listens to the silence of the mountaintop.
There is a footprint in that bog of red flowered thorns.
He's forgotten her name but it will come
when the golden boat sinks into the sea.

Growing Older

On the verge of the isthmus,
I was about to make a mistake.
The cresting waves
washing away what I know,
now changes and I can't keep up.
My mind ages and the rocks
around me are jagged, slippery,
balancing gets more difficult
as I lean into the wind, the sea
smoke of days full of chaos.

In Our Own Way

Every day the sun rises,
sometimes clouded gray, and cold.
The earth warms in its orbit
round and round
in the universe; a pattern
like our own DNA circling in our bodies,
unique.

Once I saw a picture of the universe and
of DNA side by side,
the resemblance was amazing.

Energies run in spirals, circling.
Our sun rises, our moon cycles
as the tides rise and fall
and we are one and the same
in our own way.

Journey

My journey joins the sea
weaving in and out from the land,
like a child playing tag with the waves.
Seagulls walk the lawn where
the lonely deer wanders.
The sea grasses moan in the wind,
waves reverberate on a high tide.
The light comes in sideways
on the back of the setting sun.
The days tick past,
revolve
in seasonal
repast…

Waiting for Thunder

When life is as bright as a flash
of lightning, everything
going right; the agent accepts
your manuscript, the producer
wants to make it into a movie,
you win a million on the lottery.
But you strain to hear the roiling thunder,
the fear that the storm will overtake
the bright light and darken the sky,
until that deafening rumble
takes you down…

December

(For my mother, Minnie)

The month that describes old age
sneaks up like a kitten, catches you
like a lion in claws that aren't tender.
The sun on a brief December day
glints on the alabaster skin of my
dying mother; she's not afraid.
I say a prayer with the rhythm
of her breathing, a slow rasp.
As I finish she gasps
her last breath, *amen.*
The December sun goes down
as I watch her face that no longer
appears old and fading,
the liquid light glows against her golden and
she is as beautiful as an April morning.

Acknowledgements

There are so many people I'd like to thank for the help that's been so generously given to me. The first two really made me believe my poetry should be shared. They read and edited all the work in the book and encouraged me to publish. Thank you, Judy Fitzpatrick and Bonnie Nelson.

I've driven across two states every winter to attend the residency with the Madrona Writers' group. Thank you, Bonnie, Ellie Matthews, Carl Youngman, Diana Taylor, Jenifer Lawrence, Richard Widerkehr, Bob McFarlane, Karen Seashore, Gayle Kaune, Michael and Toni Hanner, Janet Cox, Tom Aslin, Don Roberts, and David Thornbrugh for all the wonderful camaraderie while working on our writing skills.

Every summer for many years, I've attended the Centrum Writer's Conference in Port Townsend, Washington. (Thank you, Carla and Jordan for your help at Centrum.) I've had the honor to attend workshops, readings, and lectures with authors such as, Raymond Carver, David Lee, Michael Collins, James Welch, William Stafford, Marge Piercy, Jane Yolen, Richard Kinney, Marvin Bell, Lucille Clifton, John Haynes, et al. Without their influence, I wouldn't be able to put this book together.

And last, but not the least, thank you to Mary Kammer, Bill Wilkins, and Ray Gonzales who encouraged me to keep writing.

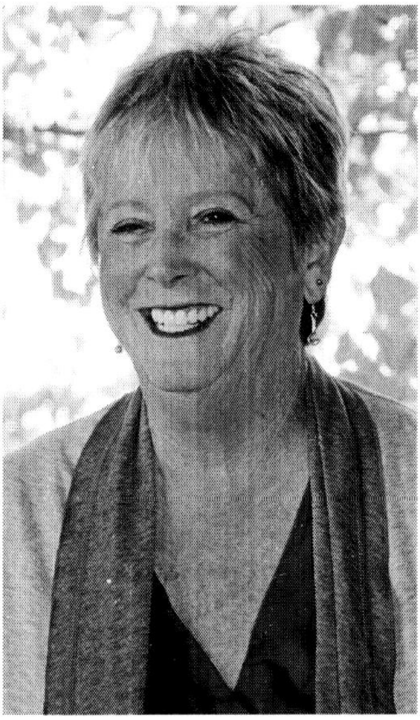

Biography

Dianne Elizabeth Butler was born to a farming family, living closely with nature and the soil on farms in Lincoln and Meridian, California, and in Enterprise, Oregon. She now lives on an organic farm in California. She loves the ocean and lived for a time on a sailboat.

She attended college after her two daughters were raised. At thirty-seven, Dianne became the associate editor of *The West Wind Review* of Southern Oregon University, and wrote for the *Siskiyou* newspaper. Also, she stage managed plays for Studio X, and made ends meet by housecleaning and working for the City of Ashland.

Her works have been published in *Cruising World Magazine*, *Bellowing Ark*, *Dream Quarterly*, *The Baja Times*, *The West Wind Review*, and other small printing presses. She just finished writing her first fiction novel.